Walking With Angels

Angelic Messages of Love to Empower Your Life

Katye Anna

D0169798

Revised Addition July 17th 2019 Copyright 2019 Katye Anna Soul Works

ISBN 9781078474382

Join Katye Anna at one of her retreats
www.katyeanna.com/retreats

More about Katye Anna:
www.katyeanna.com

Books by Katye Anna
www.katyeanna.com/books

Dedication:

I dedicate "Walking With Angels" to my beautiful angelic companions and the world of spirit. Thank-you for never giving up on me. My heart overflows with gratitude for my family, friends and students. Kathy and Lloyd, you have blessed my life since the day you were born. Mom (Kathryn Mummert) thank you for giving birth to me and being my mom. You and daddy taught me about the power of love. Steven thank you for your love and for helping me to create space and time to write. Thank you for proof reading and helping me become a better writer. I am also grateful for the love and support I continue to receive from those who have birthed into spirit especially my dad (David Mummert), sister Debbie, Allan Sethius, and Johnny.

Contents

Introduction

When I was a little girl, angels were my constant companions. About the age of nine, because of life experiences, my angelic companions began to slip away into the confines of my mind. In 1987, I experienced a soul realignment. The soul realignment I experienced got my life back on track. My entire life changed. It was like a veil had been lifted. I began to see again as I did when I was young. Slowly the angels and the world of spirit was once again front and center in my life.

I can't say I planned to "work" with angels. I guess you can say we chose each other.

In 1995, I was attuned to Reiki. I began giving people energy sessions. One day, an angel popped in to help me. Since that day more angels have popped in to help. They love helping us. My students and clients began calling me the "Angel Lady."

When an angel pops into a session I know they have a reason for doing so.

As an Intuitive Reader, I "read" my clients energy. I read what I see in their aura and chakras. A chakra will light up, or an angel will pop in, and a conversation begins between my client and myself.

The angels oversee my work. I never do a class, retreat, or reading without the angels guiding me. They also guide my life. Each angel has their own unique color ray. They send this energy into my client as I am working with them. As you read about each angel, you will be receiving angelic energy. Angels love to be of service to us. They simply want to help us heal and remember the way of love.

This book is a gift of love I give to you, my readers. I hope these different stories and meditations help you embrace that you too walk with angels.

Blessings,
Katye Anna

Chapter 1

Living In A World Of Color

Sixty-seven years ago, I was born into a world of color. I was born surrounded by angels and a host of light beings. Family members who had birthed into spirit were at my birth. My family, the doctors and nurses might not have seen them, but there were angels everywhere in that sterile hospital room when my mother gave birth to me.

This is true for every child that is born. No matter the place, era, or circumstances of your birth, you were surrounded by angels and a host of light beings when you were born. While the doctor, nurses and your parents were doing what was needed to take care of you physically, the angels and your soul were also busy.

Unlike many humans, the world of spirit never takes for granted what a miracle it is when a child is born.

Perhaps your parents planned for you.

Perhaps they didn't.

One thing is for certain, your soul planned for you to be born. Your soul created a life plan. Your parents, your family, even the location and time of your birth was planned by your soul. The stars themselves aligned with your time and date of birth, knowing that throughout your life you would need certain energies to help you on your journey.

At the severing of the umbilical cord, your soul sent forth a spark of "soul essence" into your infant body. As this occurred, your bodies of light begin to take shape and form. The consciousness of you began. The angels and light beings that gathered for your birth rejoiced. They sang out "No Greater Gift Than This Has Ever Been Born!"

The doctors and nurses worked to ensure that your mother and you were cared for during and after labor. At the same time your team of light beings and angels were grounding into the physical the spiritual form known as the light body. With each breath, your light bodies and physical form merged, giving birth to the spiritual manifestation of the soul.

Because they had forgotten, many who were present at your birth could not see the angels and spiritual beings in the room. Most could not see loved ones who had birthed into spirit hovering around. Nonetheless it is true that when you were born the angels did rejoice and you were born into a world of light. Your soul, in its wisdom, had chosen angels and guides that would be with your during your entire journey here on earth. Your angels and guides will never leave your side. They have been with you and will be with you until the day you birth back into spirit.

When I was a little girl, I lived in a world of beautiful colors. Angels were my best friends and my companions. My grandmother's garden was my favorite place on earth. It was alive with light beings and beauty.

Sadly, by the time we are eight or nine years old, the colors begin to fade into the confines of our mind. So do the angels and the world of spirit for most children. This was also true for me. I didn't realize the adults around me, and even other children, lived in a black and white world.

The angels and world of spirit that had been front and center in my world began to slip away.

Life went on. I had no idea that I was now living in a black and white world. I lived a robotic life. I didn't question what I was taught. For the most part, I followed the rules. Yes, I still experienced beauty. My relationship with God was everything to me. As a child, I experienced God through nature and going to church with my family. That said, once I started seeing the world as black and white, the world of spirit and even God wasn't experienced in the same way.

It was 30 years before I began seeing the world as I did when I was a child. After a Soul Realignment, I began to remember what I had known as a child. A Soul Realignment is a STOP sign telling you to look at your life.

Look at my life I did.

I began to question what I had been told. I began dreaming again. Not working dreams or nightmares, but beautiful dreams of angels and colorful places of light. I would travel to these places during dreamtime as well as through my thoughts and imagination. The color and the magic came back into my life. It was as if a veil had been lifted, and I could see as I did when I was a little girl. I remembered MAC. MAC is my angelic companion. He has been with me since I incarnated in this life.

The world of spirit came flowing into my life once again. Angels, Ascended Masters, Spirit Teachers and yes, those who has birthed into spirit began teaching me and revealing themselves to me.

For many years only my students, clients and a few friends knew about my connection with the angels and spiritual teachers. They called me the Angel Lady. Twenty-five years ago, people weren't talking about walking with angels or talking to people who had birthed into spirit.

I'll always remember when my brother George found out I had a special connection with Jesus. He wanted to tell people. My spiritual director asked him to keep what he had experienced to himself. He said, "George, people have been making fun of Katye all of her life. What do you think they will do if you told them that she sees angels and Jesus pops into her sessions?" My brother agreed. It would be another 12 years before I began writing my books. Only then could I freely sharing that I walk with angels and that my teachers are those who are in spirit form.

Truth is, we all walk with angels. This is why I am writing this book. I want to help you remember that you were born in a world of color. You were born with angels and light beings popping into your world.

Chapter 2

Grandma They Are Everywhere

I am a teacher of soul. I seek to teach my readers and students that we are incarnated beings. We live in a world of our own design. Through our thoughts and our emotions, we create our experiences. I believe that it is through Divine Cooperation and the spirit of Collaboration that we will find our way back to love again.

Many call me a dreamer. Perhaps I am. I dream of a world where we can all thrive. I dream of a world where we use our thoughts to create experiences of love. I dream of a world where everyone knows that Angels, Spirit Guides, Ascended Masters and the world of spirit walk among us.

Imagine what life would be like if you had never forgotten that you have a team of angels and light beings who want to help you move through your life experiences?

While it's true they cannot intervene with the choices we make, they can and do encourage us to walk the pathway of love. They whisper in our ears and visit us in our dreams to guide us as best they can. Sadly, most people wake up and have no memory of what occurred during dreamtime.

They wave red flags to try and stop us from making choices that are not in alignment with love.

Many years ago, while attending a funeral, my granddaughter Kourtney whispered, "Grandma do you see them?" I smiled and said, "Yes." She said, "Grandma they are everywhere." Her eyes were filled with wonderment as she looked around the church.

Indeed, there were angels everywhere in the church that day.

I remember telling my sister Debbie about the angels that were in the church at our grandfather's funeral. I was nine and just like my granddaughter, I could see the angels and beings of light. I remember telling my sister and she told me to be quiet. I had no idea that my sister and others could not see the angels. I now realize that many around me that day could not see the angels. Perhaps I was the only one who could see them. That said, the angels were still in attendance. They were trying to help us move through the sadness of that day.

For the most part, much of what our Angelic companions do is behind the scenes. Most people are unaware that an angel has helped them or comforted them. Most people have no idea that an angel is holding them up during times of stress. They have no idea that an angel whispered in their ear to reach out to someone. They just felt the urge to call someone. When they did, they discovered the person really needed to talk to someone. Many catastrophes have been averted because someone listened to the silent nudges of an angel. As messed up as our world and lives might appear at times, without the help of angels, spirit guides and teachers, earth and its inhabitants would have fallen into the abyss eons ago.

The good news is it's never too late to start calling on your angels for help. Although you might have forgotten about them, they have always been right by your side.

Take a moment and think how wonderful it would be if you believed that angels walk beside you. For a moment think how different your life would be if you knew that angels were with you during every experience of your life.

I know many who read my words want to believe this is true.

It is! Angels walk beside you. You have your very own team of angels. With a shift of consciousness, you can begin to live in a world where angels are a part of your life.

Angels and the world of spirit want to help you move through the experiences that happen here on earth. They can only do this if you believe they can. The world of spirit will leave signs that they are all around you. These signs just won't be on your radar. You will block them out. You will not even notice the signs because you were never taught that this was possible. Once you begin to embrace that maybe, just maybe, you walk with angels you will begin to see the signs.

Your life will change as you bring back into your awareness that you walk with angels and loved ones who have birthed into spirit can make their way known to you.

Today is a brand-new day. I invite you to embrace a new way of being in the world. Embrace that you are an incarnated soul. Embrace that angels have been with you since the dawn of your creation. Today begin to live a life guided and supported by your soul and angels.

Let's begin right now by calling upon Archangel Michael. Take a few deep breaths. With each breath begin to open your heart to Archangel Michael.

Michael brings a beautiful cobalt blue energy ray. He is the illuminator of sight. Say: *Archangel Michael, I ask that you help me see with illuminated sight. I am ready to see as I did when I was a child. I am ready to consciously walk with angels.*

Now take a few more breaths and feel the love of Michael. Take a few more deep breaths as Michael restores illuminated sight. Take another deep breath.

Focus your awareness on your third eye chakra (the center of your forehead.) Release any old outdated beliefs you have about not being able to see and hear your angels.

Take another deep breath. Trust with time you will begin to consciously bring back the light of the angels into your life. I remind you that your team of angels have been supporting your life even if you have been unaware that they have been doing so.

Take another deep breath, and continue to invite the angels into your life. Believe it or not, it's that simple. As you move through your day simply continue to invite the angels in. Welcome them into your life. Thank them for being in your life. Show appreciation.

Affirm: I *see with illuminated sight. From this day forth I consciously walk with angels. Thank you, Archangel Michael.*

With illuminated sight begin to pay attention to the signs of the world of spirit.

Here are few ways you might experience the world of spirit. As I wrote in "*Crossroads - Living a Soul Inspired Life,*" the world of spirit guides you in many different ways. Some of you **sense** the world of spirit. Some of you **hear** the world of spirit and some of you **see** the world of spirit. This is a good base to begin building your spiritual guidance system.

Here are a few ways you have all experienced the world of spirit.

You **see** a light flicker out of the corner of your eye. You **sense** that you are not alone in the room. You **feel** an energy of warmth across your face, shoulders, hands, or arms. You **feel** as if you've just been hugged. The air pressure often changes when a spiritual being enters the room. The room temperature may seem to shift, or you might catch a whiff of a beautiful fragrance that you can't quite identify.

When angels hug you, you feel a warmth flow through your entire body. Your heart expands with feelings of unconditional love. You **hear** a message to call a friend or not to go down a certain road. You **think** about someone and they call you. You have a dream about someone who has birthed into spirit (died a physical death) and you wake up with a sense of peace.

You wake up with the answer about something you had been struggling with. You wake up with thoughts encouraging you to change your life. You **hear** a thought repeated over and over again in your mind. These **thoughts** encourage you to change your life in a major way. As you reconnect with the world of spirit, you begin to pay attention to these thoughts, feelings, dreams, and guidance in ways that begin to empower your life.

Staying open to love helps us hear the world of spirit because they know only love.

As you continue reading the angel stories in this book, know that you are surrounded by your very own team of angels. Pay attention to the signs that the world of spirit is all around you. Stay open to love as you read each story. If you feel a connection to an angel message, STOP and feel the energy of the message. Trust that angels and the world of spirit can and are reaching out to you.

Chapter 3

Archangel Ariel

The Gift of Unconditional Love

The first angel I am going to introduce is Archangel
Ariel. Ariel came into my life about 20 years ago. I
remember as if it was yesterday. I was receiving an
energy session. I was in a very relaxed state when
suddenly this beautiful angel appeared. She told me
her name was Ariel. She said she was here to help me
heal my heart. She was surrounded by this beautiful
pink ray energy.

As I laid on the table receiving my energy session from my friend, swirling masses of pink ray energy began to move through me, in me, and around me. I felt lifted out of my physical body. Ariel began to send beautiful pink ray energy into me. At some point I remember crying and felt heat at my heart chakra. The experience with Ariel on that day changed my life forever.

When the healing session with my friend was over, I began telling my friend about Ariel. It's funny because to this day I remember being clear on the spelling of their name. "ARIEL," I told my friend as I spelled it. She said, "You must mean Uriel." I said, "No, she told me how her name was spelled." I repeated what Ariel had said to me. They were here to help me heal my heart. I would learn later that Ariel was also here to help heal the hearts of many other people.

During the next few weeks and months, I cried and I cried and I cried. My heart had been open by the pink ray energy of Ariel. I was healing by releasing years of experiences and memories that had blocked my heart. This was a time of accelerated healing for me. I had already found Reiki so I was already offering Reiki sessions. Ariel began to pop in when I was giving a session. Ariel took my healing work to a whole new level. I was going through huge shifts in my life. I'm not sure how I would have gotten through them without Ariel.

Through the last 20 years Ariel has been my teacher and constant companion. She opened my heart to love again. Staying open to love is our only direction. Because we were never taught as children to let go of pain, heartaches, disappointments, sadness, etc., we begin to block our lives and our hearts off from love. Through the blessings of Ariel, my heart healed. My life was transformed.

I am blessed that I consciously know I walk with angels by my side. Ariel brings beautiful pink ray energy into all my retreats, classes, and sessions. My desire is that, you too, will experience Ariel's love. As you read Ariel's message know that she is surrounding you with beautiful pink ray energy. Ariel's words are imprinted with energy.

Ariel Speaks: *"I am Ariel. I come to you at this time to aid in the healing of your heart and your world. As Katye said, I came into her consciousness over 20 years ago. That said, I have journeyed with her soul for eons. I was with her when she was born. I have stayed by her side. One day, she was ready to let me enter her life consciously. Since that day I have helped her heal. Through Katye, I have also transformed the lives of others.*

Through no fault of their own personalities forget about the world of spirit. Your childhood years offered many experiences. That angels walk among you is not one of your current day beliefs nor experiences. Nor has it been for eons. Currently on your planet there are major shifts occurring. Consciousness is shifting. Humankind is seeking to return to the way of love. This opens new portals and opportunities for Divine Collaboration. The Angelic Realm welcomes this opportunity to help humankind return Earth and her inhabitants back to a place of love.

I come to you to help you heal your heart. I know your journey has been long. Your heart holds much sadness, disappointment, and grief. During your journey you have moved through many life experiences. Intermingled with your experiences of joy and happiness are many experiences of sadness.

Please know you have never been alone.

Angels have been by your side every moment of your life.

As you read my words, please know that I am surrounding you with love. I am also sending pink rays of energy into your body and mind. Please take a deep breath. I know your journey has been long. You have loved deeply and at times you have felt deeply loved. That said, you have also felt alone and rejected by others. People have let you down. You have let others down. People have not always seen you when you needed to be seen. They have not always heard you when you needed them to hear. People you love have birthed into spirit. This has caused you much heartache.

Take another deep breath. I am here to help you begin to release the sadness. Go ahead do this now. Think about someone and/or an experience that has caused you sadness. Take deep breaths as you think of the person or experience. Give the sadness to me. You don't need it anymore. As you release the sadness from your heart, begin to also let go of the disappointment. That's it. Let go of the many times and ways others have disappointed you. Let go the many ways you have disappointed yourself. As you continue to let go I am infusing your body-mind with pink ray energy. As you read my message of love continue to allow the hurt, sadness, disappointment, and grief to leave your heart. You do not need to hold onto it. Let it go. As you continue to release and open your heart, I give you the gift of unconditional love.

On Earth unconditional love seems to be rare. I remind you that unconditional love begins with you. Begin to release the many ways that you beat yourself up for not being enough. The world of spirit sees your light. You are a beautiful beacon of light. I know you live in a world of shadow experiences. I am here to light the way and to help you remember that you are an incarnated soul. You have within you the spark of God. Take another deep breath as I continue to send forth our pink ray energy of love into your body and mind. The way to unconditional love is to love yourself unconditionally.

Everyday take some time and look into a mirror. While looking into your eyes say, "I see you and I love you." To love yourself unconditionally requires that you stop beating yourself up for not be being enough. You know the "enoughs" of which we speak. Release the judgments you and others have placed on you about not being good enough, smart enough, pretty enough, strong enough, etc. Release them.

I remind you that you have the spark of God within you. When you say "I am not enough" you are saying God is not enough. God is experiencing consciousness through you. Take a deep breath and embrace this truth. Yes, dear one, God is experiencing life through you. God in his wisdom created the angelic realm. He knew you might forget about your light as you moved through the experiences of your life. I am here to help you move through the good times and the hard times. I am here to light the way so that you can bring forth, from within, your own light. You were born to be magnificent. As you let go of the sadness, disappointment and grief, you will move out of the shadows and into love.

Please take another deep breath.

Open up to my love. Open up and be the creative force of love you were born to be. Know that you are loved unconditionally by the angelic realm and by God. This means Angels see you. Angels love you. Angels ask nothing of you. Call upon me as you move through the experiences of your life. If I am not already with you, I will be in the blink of an eye. I am Ariel. My gift to you is the pink ray energy of unconditional love."

Katye Anna: Invite Archangel Ariel into your life to heal your heart. This beautiful angel and her pink ray energy continue to help us stay open to love. Call upon Ariel to help you in times of sadness and heartache.

Your association with Archangel Ariel will bring a beautiful pink ray energy into your life and your energy field. You will literally light up the world as an ambassador of Ariel and their pink ray energy of unconditional love.

Chapter 4

Archangel Michael
The Gift of Illuminated Sight

I believe Archangel Michael is one of the most called upon angels. They are known as the Angel of Protection. While this gives people peace, Archangel Michael comes to us as the Illuminator of Sight. Michael didn't make a grand entrance in my life like Ariel did. He simply began popping in when I was working with students and clients. When Michael pops in I know I need to help the person I am working with remove the bags from their head. We all have bags.

Michael also pops into a session when the person worries a lot and has a lot of fear. The gift of Michael is that, when we see with Illuminated Sight, we understand that there is nothing to fear.

Michael brings a beautiful cobalt blue energy ray.

Many years ago, Archangel Michael began popping in guiding me to help my students and clients embrace illuminated sight. I don't think I ever give a session or teach a class, without Michael popping in.

One day, I was giving a reading to a woman. I told her I could see that she had many bags over her head. We all have bags, keeping us from seeing what is going on around us. We think the bags protect us from seeing the reality of a situation. Sadly, the bags also keep us stuck. The bags also block out our innate gift of seeing with illuminated sight.

As I continued to 'read' this woman, I could see the bags were keeping her from seeing the life she had created. I could see she was very depressed. I could see her heart was full of sadness. I also told her I could see she had chains around her feet and hands. This told me she was feeling stuck in her life. She had strong influences of archetypal energies of prostitute and victim. This told me she was negating the power of her soul for something. I could also see she believed that she had no choice in the life she was living. As I continued to read her, I could see that she was a very powerful woman. Like many people, she had given her power away, hoping that those around her would not reject her, but would love her.

As I continued reading her, Archangel Michael popped in along with Archangel Ariel. They began to infuse her body and mind with their love and healing rays. The energy of the angels softly broke through her pain and sadness. She began to open her heart to love.

When I asked her if she was ready to remove the bags she said, "Yes, but what will happen once I begin to see without the bags?" I smiled and told her without the bags she will begin to have the confidence to change those things about her life that are weighting her down and causing her depression. I also told her that without the bags she will have the courage to change her life. I told her that Archangel Michael would be by her side and she should call on him to help her.

As we continued to talk, Michael and Ariel continued to infuse her body and mind with their healing rays of love. This helped her open her heart as she began removing the bags. As she did, she began to cry. I asked her what the tears were about? She said, "For the first time in many years I'm not afraid to see."

She said, "I'm actually feeling some hope that maybe I can be happy someday." This was the gift of Archangel Michael and Archangel Ariel.

Take a few minutes and ask yourself what bags you might be holding over your head? What are you afraid to see? When you are ready, call upon Archangel Michael to help illuminate your sight. Give the bags to Michael. As you remove your bags know that Michael is infusing your body and mind with their cobalt blue energy which will begin to restore illuminated sight.

Message from Archangel Michael

Dear One, I am known to you as Archangel Michael. I come to you at this time to give you the gift of illuminated sight. I bring with me healing rays of cobalt blue energy. When you see with illuminated sight you will begin to let go of the worry and fear. With illuminated sight you will begin to see new possibilities for your life and the world you live in.

Take a deep breath and begin to open your heart to our love as we continue to speak.

Dear One, I know there are many times when you feel lost, lonely and confused. Your mind begins to play games as you allow worry and fear to overtake your thoughts. You are the master of your thoughts. When you realize that worry and fear are overtaking you, Stop, Catch and Release it.

Give your worry and fear to me.

My rays of cobalt blue energy will help illuminate your sight so you can see beyond the worry and fear.

Take a deep breath, as you, open your heart to receiving my love. Release your worry and fear.

Go ahead. Think about that which you worry about and give it to us. Take another deep breath. Begin to give me your worry and your fear. Your fear and worry have kept you frozen for far too long. Worry and fear blocks you of your joy and your peace.

I am here to aid you in the discovery that your thoughts and your emotions are the creative building blocks behind your experiences.

Breathe in the truth of our words.

We will say this again.

Your thoughts and your emotions are the creative building blocks behind your experiences.

Our gift of illuminated sight is one we give you to help you move through the experiences of your life with confidence and courage.

With illuminated sight you will have the confidence that nothing has the power to steal your joy, peace and love.

With illuminated sight you will have the courage to stay open to love despite whatever is occurring in the outer world.

With illuminated sight you can begin to embrace a peace which surpasses all understanding despite what may be occurring in your outer world experiences.

I am Archangel Michael. I have been sent to you by GOD as a constant reminder of "His" love for you.

I Am Michael. Call upon me and I will be with you instantly. Give me your fear and stay open to love.

Katye Anna: Now more than ever we need to give Archangel Michael our fear. During these times of great shifts, we are called to eradicate all fear. Give your fear to Michael. Michael will help you feel safe. Through illuminated sight Michael will help you see that no experience has the power to move you from love unless you give it the power to do so.

Association with Archangel Michael will bring a beautiful cobalt blue ray energy into your life and your energy field.

You will literally light up the world as an ambassador of Michael and their cobalt blue ray energy of Illuminated Sight.

Chapter 5

The Angel Of Death

The Angel of Death is one of the most beautiful angels I have ever seen. They light the way for those who are birthing into spirt. I'll never forget the first time I saw the Angel of Death. It was sitting on top of my aunt's house. My aunt was in the hospital. I called my mom and told her that she might want to go see Aunt Treva. I didn't tell her I had seen the Angel of Death sitting on Aunt Treva's house. This was over 26 years ago. I wasn't openly sharing about angels at that time. I did try to convince my mom to go see my aunt, but the weather was bad, and she elected to wait until morning. I knew Aunt Treva would birth into spirit before morning. She did.

I'll never forget seeing the Angel of Death that first time. It was so beautiful and seem to encompass the entire roof of my aunt's home.

We tend to associate angels with human traits like male and female. For Example - Archangel Michael is experienced as male energy while Ariel is experienced as female energy. The Angel of Death, however, doesn't feel like male or female.

I didn't realize it at the time, but I would be working with this beautiful angel to help people birthing into spirit. Since that time, I've seen the Angel of Death countless times. Walking through ICU in hospitals, working in hospice homes, and sitting by the bed of someone I loved, I have seen the Angel of Death. They are there to guide those birthing into spirit into the light. How blessed we are that this beautiful angel lights our way back into the light.

Many times, someone who is birthing into spirit has a hard time leaving the physical body. The love they have experienced while on earth makes it hard to leave. The Angel of Death does not decide when it's time to birth into spirit. They simply show up to light the way for those birthing into spirit.

I remember sitting with Johnny, a family member, as he was birthing into spirit. Leaving his physical body was extremely hard for Johnny. One morning he woke up and I asked him if he saw the angel. He said, "He did." I told him to go with it. I was crying, but I knew this beautiful angel would guide my Johnny into the light. Johnny said, "I love you." I told him I loved him and to go with the angel. He smiled at me one last time as his spirit left his body. I watched as he went with the Angel of Death into the light.

While working at a hospice house, the Angel of Death seemed to be hovering around everyone's room. Angels are not limited to being in only one place.

The people who were working on birthing into spirit could see the angels and loved ones in spirit form. They would say something to the nurses. The nurses couldn't see them. I remember teaching the nurses that those birthing into spirit see with illuminated sight. When someone you love is birthing into spirit please do your best to honor what they are telling you.

Message From The Angel of Death:

Dear One, I welcome this opportunity to dispel some of the beliefs humankind has about us. You have called me by many names, the Grim Reaper, Azrael, Mot, Kesef, and of course, The Angel of Death, to name just a few. The associations many have made is that physical death is an unwelcome experience. Therefore, I am to be feared.

While many humans do not welcome death, when seen from the eyes of the soul, death is simply a continuation of the journey of the soul. As many of you know, there is a time to be born and a time to birth into spirit.

Of course, you can hurry physical death along by choices made. When someone is leaving the physical form, I am alerted. I begin to hold vigil. Other angels are also "standing by," as are loved ones already in spirit form.

The birthing into spirit is a process much like childbirth, only now one must leave the physical form. As physical death draws closer, the person begins moving in and out of their physical form.

Physical death is determined by the lack of heartbeat. While this is true, life ends when the spirit has fully left the physical form. This process of birthing into spirit occurs on many levels even though you are unaware of it.

As the angel associated with physical death, I simply light the way through what is known to many as the tunnel of light. My light also helps those birthing into spirit leave the physical body. Of course, all of this is happening alongside whatever human experience is also occurring.

Imagine if you will: Samuel has labored hard. Life in the physical is ending. Loved ones gather by the bed side. Tears are cried, tears are held in. Watching Samuel's decline has been hard on those who love him. The room is quiet. The curtains drawn. Hushed voices trying to be brave while fearing the moment that Samuel will die.

Samuel's family is unaware that while they are having their own experience, Samuel is having his own experience. Seeing with Illuminated Sight, Samuel has been moving in and out of what many people describe as the tunnel of light.

His sight has changed. So has his hearing and many other physical senses. His awareness has slowly shifted to birthing into spirit. He may or may not be aware of loved ones in the room. He is aware of the world of spirit.

Samuel sees angels and hears angelic music as I begin to help him leave the physical form. As he moves in and out of physical consciousness, I continue to shine my light onto everyone who loves Samuel both near and far.

This is Samuel's journey. Birthing into spirit is a sacred dance. Only Samuel can decide when it is time to let go of the physical world.

As Samuel begins to let go of his physical form, I help him move into the light. Samuel is greeted by loved ones who have birthed into spirit. They gather with legions of angels to welcome him into heaven/the afterlife. Samuel, as well as his loved ones, on earth, will continued to be surrounded by angels.

Many of you struggle with the death of your loved ones.

This is especially true when they die suddenly.

I want to assure you that when your loved ones experience a sudden death, I Am there to guide them into the light.

This is also true when your loved one has taken their own life.

Many people believe they do not go to "Heaven."

This is NOT true. I light the way for everyone birthing into spirit, no matter how they have died.

After I guide your loved one, who has taken their own life, through the tunnel of light they are instantly taken by angels to a "special place of healing."

It's a peaceful place. It's a beautiful place. In this place of healing the soul spark begins a new journey.

Many times, they are unaware that they have taken their own life. As they become aware of what they did they often feel shock, and remorse. They begin to realize the ramifications of what they did. An act such as suicide implies the personality had somehow disconnected from his/her heart and soul while on earth.

During this time of healing the soul spark begins to open up to love again. They are loved and surrounded by angels, guides and ascended beings at all times. The angels sing songs of love 24/7.

During this time loved ones who have birthed into spirit are not allowed to visit. There are many reasons for this but the main one is the soul spark must be allowed to heal in their own time. Also, during this time of healing, the soul spark is not in contact with loved ones still on Earth.

As the consciousness of their soul spark heals, they begin to understand the consequences of what they did. The life plan of the soul was cut short. The dreams and visions of the soul were never fully actualized on earth. They caused pain and anguish to people they loved.

Forgiveness of self now becomes a part of the journey of the soul spark. When they are ready, through the screen of life, they watch loved ones on earth still struggling with their suicide. They must forgive themselves for the harm they caused others when taking their own life. On the soul level there is no judgement except the one we put on ourselves.

At some point the soul spark begins to venture out and is also allowed to visit with others who have birthed into spirit.

Via the Screen of Life, they continue to observe loved ones on earth. The Council of Wisdom decides when they are strong enough to attempt to make contact with loved ones still on Earth.

Do not be disheartened if you have not experienced contact with a love one who has birthed into spirit. There are many reasons for this.

Your loved one who has birthed into spirit continues to grow and evolve as they move through the many planes of consciousness within God.

Katye Anna: I wish I could draw a picture of this place of healing. It's surreal. The music of the angels is unlike anything I've ever heard here on earth.

The Angel Of Death continues. *For those of you who are moving through the experience of someone you love committing suicide, please know they are healing. You can help them by healing yourself. You do this by allowing yourself to feel joy again. You can do this with the help of angels and the world of spirit. Move through your grief, feel every raw emotion. Cry your tears. Feel your sadness. Let go of the guilt.*

Believe that given time, you can heal. You do this one moment at a time. You do this by staying open to love. When your loved one in spirit is ready, they will seek to contact you. When you are ready you will begin to allow them to do so. Forgive them and forgive yourself. Call upon the angels to help you stay open to love.

We hope this has been helpful.

I am also there for your loved ones who experienced a violent or sudden death.

Image if you will: Susan just experienced being killed. It was a violent death. At the moment of her physical death, I am there to light the way.

Many times, the human is unaware they have died. They also have no awareness both physically or emotionally about what occurred.

In Susan's case, I shielded her from remembering the experience which ended her life on the physical planes of consciousness.

Although her physical death was violent, her birth into spirit was gentle. This is true for everyone who births into spirit. Susan will continue to be supported by angels and other light beings as she begins to acclimate to life in Heaven.

Katye: Because I walk between worlds, I have been blessed to experience first-hand what happens after people birth into spirit. Consciousness continues after physical death. Everyone who has experienced a violent or sudden death is taken to a place of healing.

This is another place within God/Heaven where angels gather. They support the healing of the person who has had a violent or sudden death.

Many times, this place of healing will look like a place on earth where joy, peace and love were experienced. In this place of healing, the soul spark begins to understand that they have birthed into spirit. Having no memory of the experience that caused their death, they begin to acclimate to life without a physical body. Loved ones who have birthed into spirit play a big part helping them heal. All of this seems to happen in the blink of an eye.

There is no time on any plane of consciousness except on earth. When they understand that they are no longer on earth, and have acclimated to being in spirit, they have their past life review.

During this life review, they will see through the Screen of Life what occurred on earth. They will do so from a place of non-attachment. Those in spirit form do not have the emotions like we humans have.

The Angel of Death continues: *Yes, Dear Ones what Katye has shared is indeed true. My responsibility is to take the consciousness of the soul spark into the light. Your loved ones do not experience the pain and trauma of their physical death.*

At the instant of physical death, I am there helping them move into the light. Katye asked us to explain using an experience many refer to as 9/11. On that day many people perished. People jumped from the burning buildings.

*While I could not prevent the fear and many emotions they experienced **before** physical death, I can assure you that the **instant** they birthed into*

spirit we were there to take them into the light.
Those who died in the rubble were also taken into
the light the instant of physical death. They have no
memory of the trauma they just went through.
Many humans do not understand this truth.

Your loved ones do not experience the horror of
death in the same way you do. Upon death they go
to a place of healing. You however often think about
the way they died over and over again.

You suffer thinking that your loved ones suffered.

While it is true that during life they may have
suffered, after they have birthed into spirit suffering
ends. When they are ready to remember their
physical death, they do so without experiencing pain
and trauma.

Through the Screen of Life they watch how their
loved ones on earth are doing. When they are fully
integrated into the afterlife, they do their best to help
you know they are safe and not in pain.

If you could begin to accept these truths, perhaps
you would also bring an end to your own suffering
about the death of your loved ones. You will still go
through a period of grief and sadness, but you do
not have to suffer through this experience. Perhaps
knowing that your loved ones do not suffer after

they have birthed into spirit will help you heal your heart.

Their journey continues but without the physical form. Just like on earth there are many planes of consciousness to be experienced in Heaven/the Afterlife.

Here is a meditation to help you integrate what we have been sharing.

Take a few deep breaths. As you do, allow your body and mind to relax. You are surrounded by angels. Now begin to think about someone you love who has birthed into spirit. Continue taking deep breaths and opening your heart to love. Your loved one is safe. They are still experiencing consciousness. Your loved one loves you. They want you to be free of the sadness you carry because they no longer are with you on earth.

Take a few more deep breaths. Continue to open your heart to love.

Allow yourself to feel their love. Allow your heart to open up to this soul love.

I remind you that your loved one is still growing and evolving. They want you to do the same. As you continue to take deep breaths know that you are surrounded by angels. Allow their rays of energy to help you heal. Be gentle with your heart. Your loved one is in a place where only love abides.

Because they live in a place of love, they cannot enter into your grief. They will be close by, but it is like a door is now between you and the world of spirt. Your loved one can see you, but your grief will block you from experiencing them.

Feel your grief. Do not stay there. Your loved one has birthed into spirit. They are in a place of love.

Their time on earth may feel like it was not long enough. Truth is, humans always want more time together. The good news we give you is that, although they no longer are a part of your life physically, they can still be a part of your life. They will send you signs that they are nearby. They will do their best to let you know they are still experiencing consciousness.

I hope that my words and energy have helped you understand that I, the Angel of Death, am not to be feared, nor is death.

One day, when it is your time to birth into spirit, I will help you move from the physical into the light. Until then, embrace the love and joy that is all around you. Trust that when I come for you, or any of your loved ones, I will guide you/them into the light. Know that your loved ones in Heaven are watching over you even as they continue the grand adventure of the soul.

Katye Anna: I believe this beautiful angel should be called the Angel of Light because it is beautiful. I have learned to work over the years with this beautiful angel. I feel comforted knowing that when I see this angel, someone will be birthing into spirit guided by this angel of love.

Chapter 6

Archangel Gabriel

The Gift of Right Speech

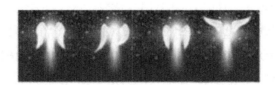

Like Archangel Michael, Gabriel just started showing up during my sessions and readings. Recently, during a reading, Archangel Gabriel popped in because my client had an overactive throat chakra. She was always giving people advice even when they didn't want it or ask for it. When triggered, she also used her words to hurt people. As I was reading her, I could see that, when triggered, she was about eight years old emotionally. They showed me that when she was a little girl her family had let her know that children were to be seen and not heard. She would be punished for interrupting the adults when they were speaking.

This made her angry, but she had no way to express her anger. As she grew older, she found that she could control others with her words.

Her words were rarely spoken in love.

This continued until the day I gave her the reading. Archangel Gabriel popped in to help her begin to heal. As I continued reading her, Gabriel began to infuse her body and mind with beautiful turquoise ray energy. This energy began to help her unravel 40 years of anger. She began to cry. Archangel Daniel also popped in and began sending in beautiful rays of golden yellow energy to help her release her resentment and anger towards her family. As the angels continued sending healing rays of energy, I continued reading her.

I reminded her that right speech was simple. I explained that if her words didn't uplift, encourage, support and were spoken in love to keep her mouth shut.

I explained to my client that it was permissible to have an unexpressed thought. I reminded her that unsolicited advice, no matter how good it was, is not good advice. While it might have made her feel good about herself, she was offering advice that people hadn't asked for. I taught her the golden rule that we should never speak when triggered.

This is true for all of us. If your words do not uplift, motivate, encourage and support others just keep your mouth shut. It's never a teaching moment if you or someone else has been triggered. It's a time for silence.

As I continued her reading, the angels' energy began to heal the wounds she carried since childhood. She cried and released years of not being heard as a child. She cried as she realized how many times she spoke in anger when she was triggered. She opened her heart to Archangel Gabriel. I told her to call on Gabriel and he would help her speak in love.

In the weeks and months following this session, she began to heal. She learned to use her voice in the ways that were in alignment with love.

Archangel Gabriel Speaks: *Dear One, I remind you that your words have power. They can be used to build up or tear down. During childhood many of you felt unheard. You were taught to be quiet. They* *saw a child, not an old soul. Many of you experienced taunting by your peers. They learned that loud voices made them feel powerful. You even had teachers and peers who put you down. You began to feel that no one could see you or hear you. You felt you had no voice. When you did get the courage to speak, many times your words were said in anger.*

I am here to help you heal.

I give you this brief meditation to help you heal.

Take a deep breath and begin to release all the times you felt silenced in your life. Breathe in my turquoise ray energy. Begin to let go of the word's others have spoken that have hurt you. Although many of these words were spoken many years ago, they continue to haunt you to this day.

Take another deep breath. As you continue to take deep breaths, release the words both spoken by others and/or words you yourself have spoken that have harmed others.

As I send my tapestry of love through you, in you and around you let go of the hurt caused by the words unspoken by others.

You have wanted to hear the words of love from another, but they did not express them. Perhaps you have also held back words of love, forgive yourself, and forgive other for not being able to tell you they loved you. They were doing the best they could at the time and so were you.

Release, let go. Open up to our healing turquoise rays.

As you move forward, call upon me to help you with right speech. Our gift to you is the art of communication. If your words do not motivate, support, encourage and are not spoken in love, reframe from speaking. You have heard silence is golden. In the silence, one can experience what words cannot convey. Call upon me whenever you need to communicate. I can help you bring forth the words that will convey what is on your heart.

I am Gabriel. I bring you the gift of the turquoise ray of light.

Katye Anna: I have been blessed to have Gabriel guide me during my sessions and readings. My words that give people strength and courage are infused with the turquoise ray and love of Gabriel. Call upon Gabriel anytime you need to use your voice. If you have been triggered, this is NOT time to talk. Just be quiet. If someone else is triggered, know that this is not a teaching moment. Remember, if your words do not uplift, motivate, inspire and encourage someone, don't speak them.

Invite Archangel Gabriel into your life to heal your throat chakra. This beautiful angel and its turquoise ray energy will help use your voice in love.

Your association with Archangel Gabriel will bring a beautiful turquoise ray energy into your life and your energy field. You will literally light up the world as an ambassador of Gabriel and their turquoise ray energy of right speech.

Chapter 7

Archangel Sarah

The Gift Of Imagination

Through Archangel Sarah, I learned that angels have a sense of humor. Archangel Sarah taught me about flow and opening up to the gift of imagination. When working with clients I'm always given a sign when a client is ready to release. Archangel Sarah shows up with dump trucks. I kid you not. Depending on how many dump trucks that Sarah brings, I know how much releasing my client must do. Archangel Sarah brings a vibrant orange ray energy. When she pops into a reading or session, I know my client has been holding onto a lot of emotions. One day during a reading, Sarah popped in. I could see that the woman I was reading had a strong archetypal influence of the Artisan. This told me that my client was very artistic and lived to bring beauty into the world.

Sadly, it had been years since she had allowed herself to be creative. She was living a life built on what everyone else had wanted her to be. Like many people she just fell into her life. She began to work with me because she knew she wanted to change her life. Looking into her energy I could see that my client had cords around her ankles and wrist. This told me she was feeling stuck in her life. Believe it or not this isn't unusual. Many people feel stuck. The good news for my client is she realized she was stuck.

As I continued to read my client, I could see that she had suppressed many childhood emotions. As a little girl she realized if the people around her were happy she was safe. This created what is known as the Pleaser Pattern. With my help my client realized she had been so busy pleasing everyone else, that she didn't know what she wanted.

One day Archangel Sarah popped into a session and began sending beautiful orange rays into my client. This energy helped my client begin releasing years of blocked emotions. Over the next few weeks we continued to explore what truly made her happy.

Up until now happiness was only a fleeting thought for my client. She began to explore what would make her happy. For the first time in her life she allowed herself to dream of creating a different life.

She made a decision to quit her job. She hadn't been happy at her job for many years. She felt this would be a step forward. She found a job where she believed she could be happy. She knew this was a steppingstone until she could figure out what she really wanted to do. Working with Archangel Sarah opened my client up to embracing passion and dreaming of what her life purpose was.

She began opening up to her creative expression and made a commitment to following her joy. About a year later she moved out West. The last time I heard from her she was teaching children how to dance. She said, she was living her dream life, had started dating and believed she had found her soul mate.

Archangel Sarah Speaks: *Dear One, you live in a world where your emotions are the fuel for your experiences. I bring you the gift of orange ray energy. My waves of light can help you release emotions which keep you stuck in your life.*

Your emotions are meant to be fluid. There are no bad or wrong emotions.

Many of you are uncomfortable with the emotion of anger. Anger is just an emotion alerting you that something is out of alignment with love.

Some of you are swallowed up by your anger because you sit in it. Without realizing it, anger became the way you expressed yourself in the world. My orange ray energy can help you release blocked emotions. When you do not acknowledge your sadness, anger, fear, hatred, and bitterness, your body and mind become blocked.

I am here to help you release the emotions that keep you trapped.

Here is a brief meditation to help you heal.

Take a few deep breaths. Open your body and mind to my orange ray energy. Release the emotions and the experiences that you hold onto. Release the sadness, anger, helplessness, and loneliness.

As thoughts rise up into your consciousness release them. Let them go. As you continue releasing, I will continue to send my orange ray energy into your body and mind. I light weave to help you remember that you are the creative force in your life. I remind you that nothing has power over you unless you give your power to that experience.

You were born to be creative.

You were born with an imagination.

Your imagination is a gift from God. Use it to create experiences of love for yourself and others.

Continue breathing. Take in my orange rays of love. Embrace that you can create a life of joy, peace and love. Use your thoughts to create a life that is expansive, a life of flow.

Release the shackles that bind you and keep you trapped in a life half - lived. Call upon us to aid you in this endeavor. Allow yourself to dream in the dreams of your soul. Open up to a life of flow. Call upon me to help you. I am Archangel Sarah. I give you the orange rays.

Katye Anna: Invite Archangel Sarah into your life to heal your sacral chakra. This beautiful angel and its orange ray energy will continue to help you embrace your creative self.

Association with Archangel Sarah will bring a beautiful orange ray energy into your life and your energy field. You will literally light up the world as

an ambassador of Sarah and their orange ray energy
of flow and creativity.

Chapter 8

Archangel Daniel

The Gift of Forgiveness

Like many of the angels, Daniel started showing up when I was giving an energy session. Daniel appears to me as a beautiful angel who emanates sunshine yellow rays of light. In my healing work, Archangel Daniel oversees the energy center known as the solar plexus chakra. Daniel pops in often during readings because they help us release resentment and anger.

During a session, Daniel popped in to let me know my client was holding onto long - held resentment toward her family. I had been working with her for a few weeks. I knew she struggled with deep rooted beliefs that she was not "good enough." She had diabetes and was literally blocking out joy. She expected people to disappoint her and they did. She also had the Rejection Pattern. She pushed away anyone who tried to get close to her. She lived in Victim energy. She also had a strong Saboteur energy guiding her life.

One day as I was working with my client, her brother who had birthed into spirit popped in. He asked me to tell his sister that he never meant to hurt her. My client rejected this, quickly saying her brother thought he could do no wrong. She told me her entire family made her feel that she was not good enough.

As I continue to read her, I saw that her brother died from cancer at the age of 17. When he died, she imprinted that everyone wished it had been her. She continued to tell herself this story until we met. She was now 49 years old. The resentment she carried for most of her life was eating away at her health, thus the diabetes.

When Archangel Daniel popped in, I asked her if she wanted to heal her broken heart and allow joy into her life? She teared up and said, "Yes, that would be wonderful, but she had no idea how to do so." This was the invitation Daniel needed from her. He began to send yellow ray energy into her body and mind.

As I continued our session, her brother tried to get her to understand that he was young when he died. He never meant for her to feel rejected by him. He explained, that he was six years older and he simply didn't want a little sister hanging around. He reminded her that she told on him and got him into trouble a lot.   When he got sick, at the age of 13, my client was only seven. By this time, she had already imprinted that she was not good enough.

The special attention he received was because he was often sick. She was too young to understand the stress both parents were under. He explained to her that their parents attempt to protect her from the harsh realities of cancer made her feel rejected and cast aside. When he died, she was 11. Again, their parents tried to protect her. They didn't take her to his funeral because they felt she was too young. They told her that her brother had died. He was in Heaven and he was an angel.

As the angels gathered around my client, I could see that she was opening up to a healing. With her brother's help, I explained that their mother experienced complicated grief and went into deep depression. Her father survived by focusing on work and disconnected from everyone. It had nothing to do with her. Sadly, she was greatly affected.

Thinking that her brother was an angel she could never measure up. The story she had told herself over and over was that her family wished she had died instead of her brother had no truth to it. She had built her entire life on something that wasn't true. She was now ready to release these beliefs.

As Archangel Daniel continued infusing his golden sun light energy into her body and mind, old outdated beliefs began to unravel. I continued to do energy work and help her with the releasing process. She began to release 40 - plus years of beliefs. Archangel Sarah sent forth orange ray energy which help her release. Archangel Ariel came in as with Michael, Raphael, and Gabriel.

Each angel brought forth their own unique ray of light and love. As my client continue releasing, she began to remember a few happy experiences with her brother. It was her brother who taught her to roller skate. It was her brother who helped her learn how to swim. As she continued to release, she made room for love to again enter in. After this session, I saw her a few more times. Her healing was amazing. She began to smile. She forgave both her parents. She realized they were doing the best they could. As for her brother, she opened her heart to his love. We worked a lot with archangel Daniel and forgiveness. She discovered that forgiveness opened up a pathway to peace and grace. She learned how to receive her brothers love.

With time she began to hear the thought forms he sent her. She began to see the signs. She said, "I feel like I have my brother back."

Archangel Daniel Speaks:

Greetings Dear One, I offer the gifts of freedom and grace. I share the following meditation.

Take a few deep breaths. Open up to my love. I begin sending into your heart my golden yellow rays of light. I encourage you to begin to release your resentment and anger.

Neither serve you.

Take a few deep breaths and begin to release the people you resent. Give them to me. Free yourself from the hold they have on you.

Your anger toward them is robbing you of your joy. In letting go of the resentment you free yourself. Your anger and resentment are eating away at you. Release your anger.

Give it to me. Release your resentment. Give it to me.

As you release, I will continue to weave a tapestry of yellow ray light into your body and mind. This yellow ray light will help you remember the way of love. As the releasing continues, simply let go of the people and experiences which are robbing you of your joy. Go ahead, let go!

Take a few more deep breaths. Begin to allow forgiveness to enter your heart and mind.

Through forgiveness and letting go of anger and resentment, your heart will be restored to right spirit.

With each breath you take, allow the energy of joy to come into your body and mind. As we continue to send yellow ray energy into your body and mind, you will begin to experience a sense of peace which allows joy into your life.

Seek joy every day. Practice gratitude every day. Stay open to love. Call upon us to help you embrace the way of love. Forgive those who have harmed you. Forgive yourself for those you have harmed.

As you continue to heal you will open a pathway for Grace to enter your life. When Grace enters your life, you will move through your experiences with love. You will understand that everyone, including yourself, was doing the best they could, at the time.

Katye Anna: Invite Archangel Daniel into your life to heal your solar plexus chakra. This beautiful angel and its yellow ray energy will continue to help you forgive others and embrace Grace.

Association with Archangel Daniel will bring a beautiful yellow ray energy into your life and your energy field. You will literally light up the world as an ambassador of Daniel and their yellow ray energy of Grace.

Chapter 9

Archangel Raphael

The Gift of Your Divine Blueprint

Archangel Raphael is another angel who pops in during my sessions with clients. Raphael comes in softly. Raphael's energy is comforting. They bring us the gift of green ray healing. This green ray energy is restorative. It brings the body and mind back into a state of harmony. When Raphael, pops in, I know my client has accepted a false belief about their physical body. This false belief has manifested as a physical disease and/or condition within the physical body. Archangel Raphael's green rays of love begin pouring into my client as I help them embrace that they have the power within their body and mind to return to a place of love. In this place of love, disease cannot exist. Where love abides illness of any kind cannot exist. When you invite archangel Raphael and their green ray energy into your life their love will gently flow into your body and mind.

Do not give energy to the disease or condition but open up to love.

Many years ago, I witnessed the power of a mother's love. One day I received a phone call from a young mother. She told me her son had been born with Spina bifida. The doctors had given this young mother a grim outlook on what his life would be like. She asked me if she should believe the doctors. I told her, if she believed the doctors, her son would become what they said. I began giving him weekly Reiki sessions.

Today he is 16 years old. He's driving a car and dating. He is an over achiever in the Paralympics games. He seeks to inspire others to be limitless. He still has Spina bifida, but he is living an amazing life.

I believe his soul chose this form as its vehicle for teaching. Archangel Raphael, the Reiki sessions, and his mother's belief, took his life from the grim outlook of the doctors to creating a life where this young man shines.

As I've said belief is everything. Sadly, we have created a planet where disease is a way of life. The good news is we are going through major shifts. I believe one of these shifts is humankind moving away from fear to a place of love. Disease cannot exist when we hold a vibration of love.

Today call upon Archangel Raphael and their green ray energy of love.

Archangel Raphael Speaks: *Greetings, Dear One, I am known to many as God's Healing Angels. While this is true my gift to you is love. As God's healing angel I am here to bring your body and your mind back to a place of love. You live in a world where disease has become a way of life for many. You do not see yourselves as spiritual beings. Therefore, when your body and mind become out of alignment, you seek to heal your physical ailments by traditional means.*

I bring to you my restorative emerald green rays. Take a few deep breaths. Breathe into your body and mind my love and healing green rays.

My emerald greens rays bring forth a remembrance of God's love. Physical disease cannot exist where love abides. Begin to breath this into your consciousness now. Take a few more deep breaths. Attune your body and mind to my emerald green rays of love. Open your heart and receive this love into every cell, tissue, and organ of your body.

Slowly, begin to feel, see, or sense this beautiful emerald green energy flowing through you, in you and around you. With each breath you take the energy swirls through you, in you and around you. Now focus your awareness on your feet. With each breath you take, begin to feel, see or experience a spiraling vortex of emerald green energy swirling around your feet. Slowly the energy flows up into your ankles, calves, knees, thighs, hips, stomach, chest shoulders, fingers, forearms, upper arms, neck, chin, face, back of head, and finally the crown of your head. The emerald green energy continues spiraling as it weaves throughout your physical, emotional, mental, spiritual bodies and your chakras. Allow yourself to meld with this energy.

This emerald green energy flows through you, in you and around you. You begin to become one with this energy. Slowly, you become attuned to the emerald green energy rays of love. The energy flows through your physical, emotional, mental and *spiritual bodies. As it does you begin to release any physical pain your body may be experiencing. You let go of the beliefs that have separated you from experiencing physical life free of illness and lack.*

As this vortex of energy spirals around you.........you let go of any dis-ease and/or condition you have created. I remind you that where love abides disease cannot exist.

NAME any disease you may be experiencing. Cast them into the swirling mass of emerald green energy. Release your fear, your anger, shame, frustrations, resentment, addictions and your pain. If you begin to see images of past experiences which have caused you pain, simply cast them into the swirling mass of energy. As the vortex of energy increases, continue to take deep breaths releasing anything that comes into your consciousness.

As I continue to fill your emotional, spiritual, mental and physical bodies with our beautiful emerald green ray energy, know that your body is being restored to the imprint of your Divine Spiritual Template. Where healing is needed, healing energy flows. Your auric field is being restored to vibrate at a rate that will support your Light Body. Continue to feel the emerald green rays of our love as it flows through you, in you and around you. Know that you are one with the Universe. You are one with Raphael. You are perfection, created in the image of God. You are a Light Being who chose to come to Earth. Embrace all the experiences that you have had here on earth as spiritual lessons.

As you continue to take in my emerald green rays of love you will begin to remember that love is the way.

Your body and mind are being recalibrated to your original divine blueprint.

This is your Divine Blueprint. Your Divine Blueprint holds the vibrational codes and frequencies of cosmic consciousness. Understand that the codes of God are within you! What God is -- you are! Love!

When you embody this truth, no disease can exist within you. In this moment nothing exists but love. This is your true state of Being. Remember this truth forever. I am Archangel Raphael.

Katye Anna: Raphael seeks to return us to the way of love. Where love is, disease cannot exist. Raphael remind us that we have the spark of God within us. We were made in God's image. This image is not a physical body but a body of light. Our physical body is the vehicle for the journey of our soul.

Without this vehicle there would be no journey of the soul. Without the spark of the soul there would be no need for a physical journey. When we begin embracing that we are spiritual beings, our diseases and health conditions will no longer exist.

I encourage you to call upon Archangel Raphael. Everyday sit in Raphael's healing emerald green ray of love. Believe that you have the spark of God within you. Believe your body can find its way back to health.

Chapter 10

Archangel Metatron

The Gift of Cosmic Consciousness

The last Angel I want to introduce is Archangel
Metatron. Using words to describe the indescribable
is what I will attempt to do. The love and gratitude I
have for Metatron is unmeasurable. I was
consciously aware of Metatron around 1999. He
entered my life and took center stage as my teacher
and guide. Archangel Metatron's energy was surreal.
If you put a thousand angels together you might

begin to understand the force and love of Metatron. To me Metatron is the king of angels. He holds the secrets of the universe and shares these teachings with those he entrusts. I've never asked why I have been chosen to be the Teacher of Soul. Perhaps it's because I love God above all others. Perhaps it's because I keep things simple. Maybe because I said yes to the call. I believe I am who my soul created me to be. Metatron chose me long before I incarnated.

In the year 2000 Metatron began teaching me. During this time, I went through many spiritual activations. I went through what was called Metatron's Fire. My life, nor I, have been the same since this spiritual activation. As a mystic, my connection to God expanded to embracing the path of love as the only path to follow. I knew that I was to continue teaching people about the world of spirit.

Metatron continues to oversee my work. He brings a golden ray energy. The golden ray energy brings qualities of unconditional love, peace, harmony and joy. If Metatron chooses you as one of his, you will go through a process of purification, receiving initiations, and moving into a time of self-actualization. As we move through these times of great shifts, Metatron's Golden Ray energy will begin to pour upon our planet. We are moving into a time of cosmic consciousness. Archangel Metatron will continue to bring forth inner truth and wisdom which will help to bring forth a new world on Earth.

Now more than ever we need to call upon the world of spirit to help us. It is time to remember that we are incarnated souls. Angels and the world of spirit are here to help us.

Archangel Metatron Speaks:

Dear Ones, May all who read my words remember that you walk with angels. May you also remember that the world of spirit is not hidden from your sight. Old outdated beliefs keep you from seeing the world of spirit. Many know this but continue to walk through life without the help they could have from the world of spirit.

My gift to you is the golden ray energy. I give you this meditation now.

Please take a few deep breaths. Open your body and mind to receive my golden rays containing peace, love and joy. As your body and mind receive my golden rays, begin to let go of the earthly experiences which have robbed you of your joy. Let go, of the pain and sadness. Let go of the resentment. Take another deep breath. Continue to open up to my golden rays of love.

My golden rays of love will begin to unravel all of the stored beliefs and fears you hold. As this unraveling continues, open your heart to allow a new rhythm to manifest within your heart. Breathe deeply and release the heartache. Release your attachment to pain and suffering, be it emotional or physical, let it go. As the golden rays of love swirls around you know that your body and mind are being reset.

I am here to help you remember the path of love, the path of peace.

While many experiences on Earth are out of alignment with love, you do not have to be.

Call upon my golden rays to help you remember your spiritual self. Attune to the energy of love and bring forth the dreams and visions of your soul.

For eons the "fight or flight" response has taken humans into patterns of fear. While "fight or flight" once served to protect you alerting you when you were in danger, over time it created a pattern of fear within your body.

Take a deep breath, as I unravel you from this energy loop that has kept your frozen in fear. Breathe deeply the golden rays of love into every cell, tissues and energy part of your body and mind.

I give you now another response to build your life upon. This is the "healing response".

When there is no real threat to the physical body or mind, you will not go into "fight or flight." You will go into a "Healing Response" instead. Your higher heart will become activated. From this place of love your body and mind will stay opened to the way of love. While the experience may be one that is emotionally uncomfortable your higher heart will alert the body and mind that it needs to bring in more light to help you move through the experience. Your lymphatic system will be activated. The energy of light will move through you, in you, and around you. This light will help to ground you. Your body and mind will stay calm and centered on love.

Breathe deeply into your consciousness my golden rays of light. Open your life to love, peace and joy.

You are loved, Dear Ones. I am here to light the way and to help you stay open to love. Call upon me. I will be with you in a blink of an eye. I leave you now with a Metatron hug. Take a deep breath as I enfold my entire essence around you. Breathe into your consciousness that you are deeply loved and cherished by God.

I am Metatron, one who oversees the Angelic and the Earth Planes of Consciousness.

Katye Anna: Invite Archangel Metatron into your life to help remind you that you are loved and cherished. This beautiful angel and its golden ray energy will help you embrace that you are an incarnated soul.

Association with Archangel Metatron will bring a beautiful golden ray energy into your life and your energy field.

You will literally light up the world as an ambassador of Metatron and their golden ray energy of love.

Chapter 11

Stay Open to Love

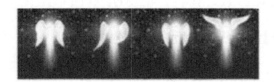

I hope that my angel stories have given you a new understanding of just how loved you are by them.

We all walk with angels.

Their love for us is unconditional.

They simply want to help us walk through the many experiences of our lives. In truth, we will never know how many times they have helped us during our lives.

Help us they have and help us they will. Their energy rays can heal us. Their messages of love can transform our lives.

We are living in times of great shifts. Many people are living in fear. I believe, now more than ever, we need to call upon the angels to help us. If we are to return our world and its inhabitants back to a place of love, it is going to take all of us working together. This means those of us in physical form as well as our companions in spirit form.

I invite you to join me in creating a world where the spirit of Divine Collaboration and the Spirit of Cooperation is the forefront of everything we create.

Use the Three Spiritual Keys:

> *Converge in love.*

> *Take responsibility for your thoughts and emotions.*

> *Embrace that we can only succeed together.*

Stay open to love and know that every experience here on Earth is a temporary one.

Learn to let go of the past.

When you wake up in the morning know that it is a new day. Live in gratitude and trust that your angels and your soul are with you every step of the way.

Every day call upon the angels to walk with you.

Talk to them.

Treat them like you would your most beloved friend.

If you don't know what angel you need, just say *"Calling all angels, I need help with_____. "*

Call them – they will come. In a blink of an eye they will be by your side. Trust that they know how to help you even without you telling them what you need.

Enjoy walking with angels. Here are a few things to remember when walking with angels:

• Angels are messengers sent forth to share the light

• Angels have no desire to be worshipped

• Angels love us and simply want to help light our way during our life.

• Angels really do not look like humans but appear to us in ways we need them to.

• When people birth into spirit, they do not become angels. They feel angelic. They continue to watch over us, but they do not become angels. Angels are on a different pathway than those of us who have souls. (Enoch is the only human who became an angel after physical death. He is known as Metatron.)

• Angels can only intervene when it doesn't go against the plan of the soul or the free will of the person. They can encourage you and nudge you toward making a different choice. At the end of the day you are the creative force behind your life and choices.

• Through Divine Collaboration with angels and the world of spirit, we will find our way back to love.

• The Angel of Death is beautiful and gently guides us back into the light when we birth into spirit.

• Angels do not have gender. We assign human traits to them. They are okay with this.

• Everyone has a Guardian Angel. Calling in your Guardian Angel is easy. Simply say, "*Guardian Angel, I open my heart and invite you into my life. Surround me with your love. Please make your way known to me in ways that I can understand. Please guide me and direct me. Help me to move through my life in love.*" Do this connecting prayer every morning. Invite your guardian angel into your life as you move through your day. As you begin to connect with your guardian angel you might learn its name.

Don't force the name. It will pop into your mind when you least expect it.

• Angels cannot stop humans from making choices that are not in alignment with love.

• Angels have a beautiful sense of humor.

• Angels are not fairy godmothers. They are not here to grant your wishes. They are here to help you. They are here to guide you. In times of stress and heartache they are here to help you heal by sending you their healing rays of light.

One way angels communicate with us is through thought transmissions. You **hear** a message to call a friend or not to go down a certain road. You **think** about someone and they call you. You **have** a thought repeated over and over again in your mind. Sometimes these **thought transmissions** encourage you to change your life in a major way. Over time you will learn to trust these thought transmissions.

Take a few minutes now and think about thought transmissions you may have received from an angel.

Here are more ways you may have experienced an angel. You **see** a light flicker out of the corner of your eye. You **sense** that you are not alone in the room.

You have **felt** an energy of warmth across your face, shoulders, hands, or arms.

You **felt** as if you've just been hugged. Air pressure changes when a spiritual being enters the room. The room temperature may seem to shift. You might catch a whiff of a beautiful fragrance that you can't quite identify.

When the angels hug you, you feel a warmth flow through your entire body. Your heart expands with a feeling of unconditional love. They leave a penny, a feather, or some object for you to find.

Tale a few moments and think about a few ways you have experienced an angel.

Angels don't need you to know their name. They will answer to whatever name you give them.

Angels have no agenda of their own. They simply want to help you move through life here on earth.

Angels can be everywhere and nowhere. They are not limited to time and space in the same way most humans are.

Today I invite you to become an ambassador of light and help the angels light up our world with the many energy rays of color. Your life and our world will never be the same. *Katye Anna –The Teacher Of Soul*

ANGEL	ENERGY RAY		GIFT
ARCHANGEL ARIEL	PINK	CALL UPON ARIEL IN TIMES OF GRIEF AN, SADNESS AND HEARTACHE.	UNCONDITIONAL LOVE FOR SELF AND OTHERS
ARCHANGEL RAPHAEL	EMERALD GREEN	CALL UPON RAPHAEL FOR PHYSICAL HEALING	COMMUNICATING IN LOVE
ARCHANGEL GABRIEL	TURQUOISE	CALL UPON GABRIEL TO HELP YOU WITH RIGHT SPEECH	AWAKENS YOUR DIVINE TEMPLATE
ARCHANGEL DANIEL	YELLOW	CALL UPON DANIEL WHEN YOU ARE READY TO LET GO OF RESENTMENT AND ANGRY	GRACE AND PEACE
ARCHANGEL SARAH	ORANGE	CALL UPON SARAH WHEN YOU ARE FEELING STUCK	AWAKENS YOUR CREATIVITY AND FLOW
ARCHANGEL MICHAEL	COBALT BLUE	CALL UPON MICHAEL WHEN YOU ARE IN FEAR OR WORRY	ILLUMINATED SIGHT
ARCHANGEL METATRON	GOLD	CALL UPON ARCHANGEL METATRON WHEN YOU NEED SPIRITUAL GUIDANCE	INNER TRUTH AND WISDOM

THE THREE SPIRITUAL KEYS
FOR EMPOWERED SOULFUL LIVING

Key One:
CONVERGE WITH OTHERS IN LOVE.

Key Two:
TAKE RESPONSIBILITY FOR YOUR THOUGHTS AND EMOTIONS.

Key Three:
WE CAN ONLY SUCCEED TOGETHER.

Katye Anna

TEACHER OF SOUL

www.KatyeAnna.com

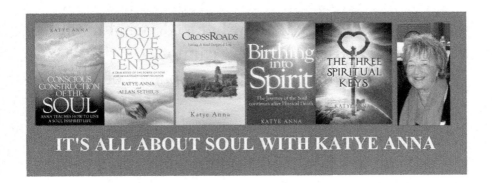

IT'S ALL ABOUT SOUL WITH KATYE ANNA

About the Author

For over twenty-five years, Katye Anna has been sharing her spiritual gifts and messages of transformation and empowered soulful living with people around the world. Katye Anna is a Teacher of Soul, transformational author, speaker, and retreat facilitator. She embraces life as a mystical, magical, and spiritual journey. She chooses to consciously walk with God.

Gifted with the ability to travel the many planes of consciousness within God, Katye Anna walks between worlds. Angels are her teachers and companions.

Katye Anna has a direct connection to the world of soul and the world of spirit. Communicating with the world of spirit is as natural as breathing to her.

Katye Anna writes and teaches from her heart. Her gifts of travel and sight allow her to do what many authors and spiritual teachers cannot do - give firsthand descriptions of the many planes of consciousness within God.

When she writes about the Tunnel of Light, she writes from her firsthand accounts of helping people move into the light. When she writes about her sister Debbie's cabin in heaven, she can describe it in detail because she spends time with her there. When Katye Anna describes the Hall of Records where souls gather together to finalize soul agreements, she is describing it as she has seen it during her travels. Katye Anna uses her connection with the world of spirit to share the teachings of Anna. In 2013, Katye became the voice for Anna (thus the name Katye Anna). Anna is a group of 976 souls who no longer experience consciousness on earth. Anna teaches from the higher planes of consciousness and seeks to bring forth teachings that will help personalities take responsibility for the energy they bring to earth and their experiences.

The insight from Anna is endless. Katye Anna's books, classes and retreats offer teachings and guidance meant to help shift people's awareness about being incarnated souls.

Further, her work illustrates how our experiences here on earth are just a small part of the journey of the soul. Katye Anna provides teachings and experiences to help clients and students release old outdated beliefs and patterns. Once that is accomplished, they are able to lead empowered lives fueled by one's soul and the universe.

Together with Anna, Katye teaches students and clients how to consciously connect with their own soul, angels, guides and the world of spirit.

Katye Anna believes everyone has a direct line to the world of spirit. Through meditations and spiritual guidance, Katye Anna opens those she works with to embrace their own unique line of communication with the world of spirit. With her messages of love, she seeks to show that everyone can live an empowered life.

Information

For information about Katye Anna's ongoing classes and retreats go to: www.KatyeAnna.com

To contact Katye Anna for speaking engagements email her Katye@katyeanna.com

Want to sign up for Katye-Anna's very popular ONLINE **Mind Mastery Class**? Go to Mind Mastery

Follow Katye Anna on Facebook:

https://www.facebook.com/KatyeAnna

Book a private session over the phone or locally in person with Katye Anna:

https://www.katyeanna.com/private-sessions

Books By Katye Anna

The Three Spiritual Keys are offered by Anna to teach humankind about personal responsibility in what we are creating. Daily use of The Three Spiritual Keys will lead you onto a pathway of consciously creating your experiences in love. Conscious Creators use right speech to motivate, encourage and inspire other to action. They live from the heart and are guided by soul.

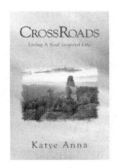

CrossRoads-Living A Soul Inspired Life In this revealing and engaging book, Katye Anna shares about soul realignments, angels guiding her, her dark night of the soul, spiritual activations, soul love and much more as she tells her story of transformation. She shares how her soul began to guide her via her dreams and thought transmissions as she released old outdated beliefs.

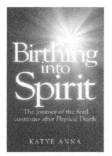

Birthing into Spirit shares the story of six teachers as they birth into spirit. The stories shared offer insights and gifts from those birthing into spirit. Their hope, visions of the afterlife and their faith that dying a physical death is not the end of their stories, are clearly expressed. This book will teach you how to help someone you love as they birth into spirit.

Conscious Construction of the Soul is a ground-breaking book that reveals how the soul is created and how it journeys through lifetimes. You will learn about soul contracts and agreements. Anna will teach you about Soul Parenting, Dreams and Astral Time, Higher Centering Children, and much more. This book is for you if you are ready to live a soul inspired life.

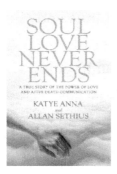

Soul Love Never Ends is the true story of Katye and Allan Clark and how their love continues even after Allan's physical death. By reading this book you will learn about soul love, after-death communication and how your loved ones who have birthed into spirit try to communicate with you.

Tell Them – Messages From the World of Spirit

Katye Anna shares inspiring stories from loved ones who have birthed into spirit. She shares the many ways those who have birthed into spirit seek to communicate. She offers insight how you too can connect with your loved ones now living in the place many call Heaven.

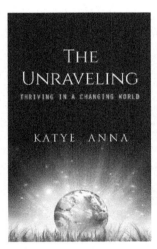

The Unraveling – Thriving In A Changing World

Katye Anna offers insights that will help you wake up and begin to take responsibility for what and how you are creating your experiences. She shares how personal responsibility, imagination and following one's intuition are tools for transformation.

Visit Katye Anna's Author Page

https://www.amazon.com/Katye-Anna

Every year in the Spring, Katye Anna leads a life transforming five-day spiritual retreat at the Mago Retreat Center outside of Sedona, Arizona.

You are invited to join her at the next retreat. Bring a friend or partner along to share this amazing experience!

Click here for more information: Mago Retreat

Please help Katye Anna get her teachings of love out to others. Go to Amazon.com to leave a review of her books. LIKE and FOLLOW her on Facebook. SHARE her Facebook page with friends and family.